ANNE AWBREY

Copyright © 2015 Anne Awbrey

All rights reserved.

ISBN-10: 0692370366
ISBN-13: 978-0692370366

DEDICATION

My collection of poems was inspired by Our Father, His Son, and the Holy Spirit. Without their love and guidance, none of these verses would exist today.

To my husband Richard. His enthusiasm, love, and support have been my main stay in this effort.

To my son Brett and always my Little Buddy. You are the major force in the completion of this project. The faith and love you have for me is tremendous.

To my daughter Paige, my son Rick, and their families. A big thank you for inspiring the deepest love and appreciation I have in my heart for family.

To my dearest friends Carole & Rich. Your journey has inspired me. I have the upmost love and respect for both of you.

To Susan, Val, and Sally. A huge thank you for listening and always being there for me with encouragement and support.

To Ann Duelke and Jim & Joann Garst. Your strong spiritual conviction and encouragement are essential to me. We can make a difference in people's lives.

CONTENTS
"BELIEVE"

Prologue	*vii*
I know your fear and pain	*8,9*
A closer walk with Thee	*10*
Where are the answers?	*11*
Heavenly Father	*12*
Each day	*13*
Praying for guidance	*14*
I can take charge	*15*
God's gifts	*16,17*
God's child	*18,19*
Awareness	*20,21*
God's presence	*22*
Gratitude & Love for our creator	*23,24*
Is there a miracle?	*25,26*
Hand in hand forever	*27*
A Thanksgiving wish	*28,29*
Heaven awaits	*30*
Close to Him	*31*
Endless love	*32*
Examine your sorrow	*33,34*
Father in Heaven	*35,36*
Footprints in the sand	*37*
Forever at my side	*38*
Forgive	*39*
Heavenly Father	*40*

CONTENTS
"BELIEVE"

To go forward	*41*
Can you hear me Father?	*42,43*
You are my strength	*44,45*
His light will never dim	*46*
I will walk with God	*47*
Love	*48*
March with me	*49,50*
March with God	*51,52*
Miracles	*53,54*
Our Lord and savior	*55,56*
Praise God and His glory	*57,58*
The path you choose	*59,60*
Your reward	*61,62*
To live as you faithful servant	*63,64*
The secret place	*65,66*
The wonder of today	*67*
Truth & light	*68*
Together	*69,70*
Walk with me	*71*
Walk with the Lord	*72*
Why believe?	*73,74*
Your are not alone	*75,76*
Your promise forever	*77,78*
Your way is my way	*79*
Can you hear me Father	*80*
Our greatest fear	*81*

CONTENTS
"GRIEF"

To say goodbye	*82*
Fear of tomorrow	*83,84*
Guidance	*85,86*
I give my heart	*87*
My child my angel	*88,89*
My evening prayer	*90,91*
My walk alone	*92,93*
Prepared for tomorrow	*94*
Until we meet again	*95*

"ABUSE"

A five year olds fear	*96*
A heart as good as gold	*97,98*
Always with me	*99,100*
Friend	*101*
I'm safe with you here	*102,03*
To change my life	*104,05*
Who I Am	*106,07*
A victim no more	*108,09,10*
Get help & get out	*111*

"ABOUT THE AUTHOR"

My promise	*112,13*
My story	*114,15,16*

PROLOGUE

Today when you are suffering from feeling alone, grief, pain, or fear that are weighing heavy on your heart, remember God is with you! God is waiting to communicate with you and to help you find the answers you are looking for. God will affirm with you His words to help you through the crisis. His love for you is ever present. You have been created in His image and likeness. God longs to spend time with you.

The journey you are walking can transcend into a meaningful relationship with God. If you allow Him to guide and walk with you, your life will change. Fulfillment and joy will enhance your life from this day forward. You can emulate His love and goodness in your life going forward. We can and should make choices that will enhance, not hinder our lives.

Embrace the good in life and cast out the negative that is pulling you down. You are not powerless and you can overcome adversity. Rise above the sadness and despair and walk with God. There is goodness and beauty waiting for you today. Speak and He will hear you. Listen and He will answer and give you guidance. He is there to be your constant companion and will never let you down. Surrender to God today, Survive tomorrow. Your life will be changed forever!

I KNOW YOUR FEAR AND PAIN

I know your fear, I know your pain, and I have walked your road before. In the midst of sadness, I knew there would be more.

I've cried your tears so many times and often felt despair, this hand that was dealt to me was wrong and so unfair.

I had no hope, I didn't care, my life was over then.
No will to face tomorrow, I'd never be happy again.

A constant state of fog prevailed each and every day.
To think about a future alone, I pondered in dismay.

I couldn't think, I couldn't plan, and had no inner drive. He was gone, I missed him so, and why was I alive?

The hours and days passed, an answer yet to find.
The sun would shine, I'd hear the birds, and yet I was so blind.

To feel that sweet tomorrow, as life proceeds each day. To take a breath and stand as one, to never look away.

I had a life, I have a life, it's changed somewhat it seems. I lived a life, yet will go on with brand new hopes and dreams.

For as they say life changes without a guarantee.
To anyone… that you can count on, just what you want to see.

It's hard to see tomorrow without the one you love.
If you believe and trust in God …HE listens from above.

Psalm 119:35 - *Direct me in the path of your commands, for there I find delight.*

A CLOSER WALK WITH THEE

Raise your hands and praise His name, our Lord and heavenly Father. Your life is blessed because of Him. Our God is King, creator of all; we know there is no other.

Although we falter and sometimes fall from His grace with eyes that do not see, in quiet hours we acknowledge our sins and kneel in prayer to thee.

And He forgives and puts His trust that we will find the way, to walk the road He has for us each and every day.

It can be very difficult to be as He would be,
to turn our backs on sinful acts and live life selflessly.

If we could bask in His true love and live by His example,
I do believe that we would live a life that's more than ample.

We recognize our blessings yet often pray for more.
Are greed and ego stopping you from walking through His door?

For once the door is open you will clearly see, that your life will be completely full with a closer walk with Thee.

Genesis 17:1- Now when Abram was ninety-nine years old, the LORD appeared to Abram and said to him, "I am God Almighty, Walk before Me, and be blameless

WHERE ARE THE ANSWERS?

I am living a life that is less than the way, I was taught to grow up in the world of today.

I have questions without answers, I'm searching for right. In the midst of this darkness, will there be light?

My life just continues on a lonely path, I struggle with existence and with the wrath.

From the anger confusion remains, a life that is wrong for me and causing me pain.

I look for answers from God's holy work; they just don't come clearly when I look. I know that he speaks with a loud voice, whether to follow and hear is certainly my choice.

I sit with my pity and wait for his word, to enlighten and teach me the way to be heard.

It's obvious to me now that I carry this burden, to share with my partner and never to hurt him.

As time moves on now I continue to wait, for the answers that come will determine my fate. I will put faith in God our heavenly Father; solutions will follow in one way or another.

HEAVENLY FATHER

Heavenly Father I'm now all alone, in a place full of memories that we called home.

Every corner I turn I see Him here, I can carry on as one without any fear.

There are pictures and things within these four walls, my energy is drained as evening falls.

I haven't been alone for forty plus years, I'm confused and overwhelmed now overcome with my tears.

Give me the courage and faith that I need, to challenge myself as one going forward alone indeed.

Although their death is something I never expected, we all can stand tall and be resurrected.

I am strong and capable of handling my life; I can do it well without any strife.

I will continue to listen and know when I pray, you are walking beside me every day.

You won't let me falter and won't let me fail, the future is mine and your love prevails.

John 8:12 - *When Jesus spoke again to the people, he said, "I am the light of the world. Whoever follows me will never walk in darkness, but will have the light of life."*

EACH DAY

Each day as I awaken, I thank the Lord for what today will bring. I count my blessings and look to him his teachings are everything.

My heart rejoices as I look for joy and contemplate this great new day. Without our Father in my life, I would walk a very lonely path without purpose along the way.

My life is very complete as I give praise to Christ my savior. With my love and trust in him I will never waiver.

He gives life true meaning to his people and clearly leads their way. A bond of Christianity and righteousness for his humble servants each and every day.

When you awake tomorrow with love, please pledge to walk him. Your life will hold the answers and his light will never dim.

PRAYING FOR GUIDANCE

I am praying for guidance and I know you are here, you are constantly with me I will abandon all fear.

With your love and presence I am now whole, I relinquish my need to possess and control.

My experience tells me that your answers come, with prayer and conviction when the day is done.

I trust and believe in your will Lord for what happens to me, I will strive forever to walk the path chosen with thee.

It's sometimes a rough road and the purpose seems bleak, in the quiet I listen for words that you speak.

Until today Lord with my past not taken for granted, your words, love, and greatness keep my feet firmly planted.

In life there are challenges it is very probable, yet with your love and guidance all things are possible.

John 16:13 - However, when he, the Spirit of truth, is come, he will guide you into all truth: for he shall not speak of himself; but whatever he shall hear, that shall he speak: and he will show you things to come

I CAN TAKE CHARGE

I can take charge and make my way; I never needed *anyone* to plan my days.

I took charge of things from an early age. Watching my Mom and sister I would never engage with anyone who would challenge me or change my life from what I knew it should be.

When problems arose I managed them well, no need for help now and no need to tell.

Anyone who might suggest other ways, to alter my life and change my days.

I want to be happy and financially secure. It's in my hands now of this I am sure.

As we walk down the path of life's destiny, I know it is good and left up to me.

Problems that would happen along the way, when I take charge they will go away.

Romans 8:33 - Who will bring any charge against those whom God has chosen? It is God who justifies.

ANNE AWBREY

GODS GIFTS

The brilliant green leaves on the trees, the babbling of a brook. The eagle soaring on his winged flight, how often do we look?

The whispering of grasses in the fields so very near. The warbling of a meadow lark, how often do we hear?

The quiet in the still of night, stars shining high above. The kindness and goodness when received, is it recognized as love?

The wonder of a child's birth, the tranquility of death. The passing of each wondrous day, do we pause to take a breath?

A golden grain of sand, purple mountains majesty. Frothy waves as they crash on shore, how did they come to be?

Children think these things when growing up and often question why. Can we gaze in true amazement now, or will we even try?

Or should we be complacent, wander aimlessly on our way. Or treasure each and everything we witness every day.

Let's stop and smell the roses…don't delay this time. Look around and be grateful for life, because this life is so sublime.

The very gifts God gives us are just outside your door. They're beautiful and incredible how could we want for more.

1 Corinthians 12:1- Now concerning spiritual gifts, brethren, I would not have you ignorant

GOD'S CHILD

Each day as I awaken I find gratitude and love, for each challenge I will face today I look to you above.

For as I've grown with years behind me now I realize one thing, a bright new promise to us is what you always bring.

And as I wait for answers my future now is clear, I feel your presence always and know that you are here.

I cannot understand and surely have some fears; I pray to you for help your answers muted by my tears.

Please help me know today that the choice is in your hands. And though the choice seems hard for me, I know your answer stands.

Before my needs, thus stifling the future that I have planned, yet when I pray for answers I am cradled in your hands.

I can't doubt you Father, I have to see this through. When your choice is final, I am not alone, I always will have you.

And so I face the chapter in my final walk through life. I am ready to walk with you without the pain and strife. I trust the words you give me, the purpose of my walk, I need to trust you Father, to listen now, not talk.

I am on my knees and wiser now, as you have shown to me.

Clearly a child of God, to walk with Him is where I need to be.

Matthew 5:9 – Blessed are the peacemakers, for they will be called children of God

AWARENESS

Today there's awareness for me that is not entirely new, life doesn't always happen the way that you want it to.

We all have dreams of how things should be; the bubbles are bursting and there is disappoint for me.

I am not in control and need to accept who's running this show, it's not something new and we all should know.

Our Father guides us and teaches us all, to walk His journey as planned, if we don't we fall.

This lesson we failed to learn we will have to repeat, yet once learned a second time can be bitter sweet.

For the ones that we love it's hard to let go, to not step in and try to control.

We watch from the sidelines and pray for their strength, to accomplish what God wants at any length.

They have always been His as the Holy Scripture states. It's in God's hands now and nothing equates to their happiness, when walking the journey with Him.

To find inner joy, the Father, Son, and Holy Spirit with love to employ.

On their faithful subjects whose lives will project, love, gratitude, and worship with deepest respect.

For all those around them to witness and praise, joy, happiness, and fulfillment for the rest of their days.

GOD'S PRESENCE

I am right here with you. I never will be far from you, just reach out for guidance from me.

I pledged to you always and live by my words, that if you need me your prayers will be heard.

I solemnly promise as I did from the start, my love and my blessings carry deep in your heart.

For when you are tempted to live without faith, a life without me will create great dismay.

For failure and tragedy will always prevail, leaving you with a life that will fail.

Breaking your spirit and a need to exist, open your heart and spirit to me now, most cannot resist.

To believe in my love and the miracles I give, embrace these great wonders all the days that you live.

With my truths and lessons always present for you, I am here forever in all that you do.

GRATITUDE & LOVE FOR OUR CREATOR

I am feeling rather down today and cannot tell you why. The sky is the bluest of blue today not a cloud is in the sky.

I know that when I haven't rested well on the night before, it's hard to keep my optimism in tact within an open door.

To stay on track and give you praise to be thankful for all things, to know just how great this life is and what its wonder brings.

To look for you in everything with gratitude and love, awareness of what is my daily bread sometimes needs a shove.

When time allows, turn around be sure to recognize. God always demonstrates his love for you just open up your eyes.

And as this day closes give praise on bended knees, tomorrow will be better, go forward with due ease.

Embrace each glorious moment and be grateful all day long. Speak His words to all you meet and know that you belong.

As one of his students to share his love, to give each person that you meet a chance to look above.

To witness his greatness and embrace his faith for you, so spread the word and pass it on and do what you can do.

Each day that follows will be fulfilled and yours alone to keep, so wake each day with gratitude and blessings you will reap.

Psalm 103:20 - *Praise the LORD, you his angels, you mighty ones who do his bidding, who obey his word.*

IS THERE A MIRACLE

Our Father in heaven I'm now on my knees, praying for guidance and understanding, can you hear my plea?

I fail to see why my friends have to struggle. As sickness and death loom over their lives, causing pain, heartbreak, and trouble.

I firmly believe that when prayers are heard, clarity comes to us in your profound words.

You never abandoned me or left my side, I rely on you always to be my guide.

When there is doubt, with a miracle requested, I wonder quite frankly will it be given or will they be tested.

The word itself can be interpreted to be, with more than one purpose for those who will see.

For if one knows miracles they should recognize clearly, the choice is yours; you perform miracles without condition to all you hold dearly.

Every life lesson learned is a true miracle to me, when called up to heaven, entering through the gates, the wiser you'll be.

You are given a chance as life slips right on by, to repent and ask for forgiveness, no need to clarify.
Our Father forgives and will cleanse your soul, and when your time comes, you will once again be whole.

To join all the others who have passed before you, look ahead with joy now and know that it's due.

To stand with the angels and proclaim your love, with the Father, Son, and Holy Spirit in heaven above.

Proverbs 21:31 - *The horse is made ready for the day of battle, but victory rests with the LORD.*

HAND IN HAND FOREVER

Today is the day we stood hand in hand; we pledged life together with our wedding bands.

To face our tomorrows, to grow together with each day that we live. To laugh with, to love with, and sometimes forgive.

For life isn't perfect we knew from the start, forever together we pledged with our hearts.

For rich or for poor, in good times and bad, the pledge that we made then, was all that we had.

Our love has not changed throughout all these years; we should always look back, without regret and without tears.

As time slips away our goal now is clear, walking Gods path and trusting His guidance without doubt or fear.

Our love always with us we pledge to the end, my partner forever and my very best friend.

When our time on earth has ended, in His Holy Kingdom we stand hand in hand.

Job 29:2 - *"How I long for the months gone by, for the days when God watched over me,*

ANNE AWBREY

A THANKSGIVING WISH

My wish is for the world to live without being judgmental.

To live without greed.

To put others before their own ego and to recognize that ego can be eliminated for a happy life.

For people to learn to forgive others.

For people to be thankful for the good in their lives.

For people to appreciate friends and family.

For people to be respectful and compassionate.

For people to pass on to others laughter, love and appreciation.

To look at our past and glean the good from it.

For people to recognize that individuals are different, but basically need the same thing ….. love.

For the world to express love and gratitude to their fellow man.

For people to praise God for the blessings they have now and will continue to receive.

For the world to be grateful for God's unconditional love.

For people to love God unconditionally and to recognize and live by His righteousness and truth.

Adoration
Confession
Thanksgiving
Supplication

HEAVEN AWAITS

I look in true amazement at the brightest blue of skies, I glance around the hillside at miracles right before my eyes.

My thoughts drift so swiftly to a world in which there's love, abounding from the rooftops in his glory from above.

This world is old and tired now and dreadfully abused, with dissention and war between us, no winners all will lose.

His words so clearly spoken have been lost along the way, as restless souls we look for more , yet we have no time to pray.

Heed His words and kneel in prayer as He would want you to, He suffered, died and rose for us, so now it's up to you.

Walk tall and face adversity, His words your sword and shield. Cast out all the evil in life, his coming will be revealed.

A glorious heaven waits for us so stand together strong, to meet our Father once again and be where we belong.

CLOSE TO HIM

Close your eyes, feel his presence, listen to Him speak.

Know He's there right beside you, the answers you may seek.

Be still and feel Him comfort you. Adjust to peace, contentment, truth, and love, now you need to trust.

His promise has been there for us this entire time; create your world today with love to live a life sublime.

Remember that He will spare his children the anguish of hurt and pain. In glory, He will return to us and we will be whole again.

Matthew 11:28-30 - Come to me, all you who are weary and burdened, and I will give you rest. Take my yoke upon you and learn from me, for I am gentle and humble in heart, and you will find rest for your souls. For my yoke is easy and my burden is light.

ENDLESS LOVE

There is endless love in my heart today, a love so great it is difficult to convey.

To look at someone passing by, to know there are loves that have gone awry.

I want to shout "Just feel His love," and cast the hurt aside. I cannot find the words to share; the need is often too much to bear.

We have so much to be grateful for; we speak of love so often, but just cannot give more.

As though we are afraid to reach within our soul, and find original love that was given years ago.

His pureness and goodness we were blessed with at birth, to share and feel this wondrous love, what would it all be worth?

Reach out today and take the risk and say, I am your likeness, I love, believe, and will take time to pray.
For those who will not walk the road of happiness, love, and show faith. Pray for them today, for this greatest gift of life is our Father up above.

John 14:23- Jesus answered and said unto him, If a man love me, he will keep my words: and my Father will love him, and we will come unto him, and make our abode with him.

EXAMINE YOUR SORROW

Examine your sorrow and let go of your grief, they have entered the Kingdom and are whole once again, can you feel some relief?

Together forever your forever is gone, I feel lonely and sad now, whatever went wrong?

Forever is only a heartbeat away, step out of the darkness and go on your way.

As one chapter closes another will start, if you feel God's presence deep in your heart.

We left behind our living with pain, while walking this path there is nothing to gain.

That we recognize now as a lesson well learned, our almighty Father would not leave without return.

He is always with us and tempers your fear; our Almighty is with you his words loud and clear.

The devil will tempt you and challenge your life, forsake the temptation forge on without strife.

Tomorrow's your future they'll always be near, a love that's forever, to always revere.

They loved you completely and know who you are, your strong and are free now to follow your star.

You cannot give up and continue to grieve; walk forward now, just believe.

That God gives us answers when things are not clear, be quiet and listen the answers you'll hear.

God loves all his children and leaves you as one, to find a new future without fear and longing as your new day's begun.

That one love is precious and will always be, a part of forever between you and me.

Psalm 116:9 - *that I may walk before the* LORD *in the land of the living.*

FATHER IN HEAVEN

Father in heaven I am waiting to hear, that you will protect me and banish my fear.

I lay in the darkness of my lonely room, I listen to fighting, this feels like a tomb.

Tear after tear I shed as I lay in my bed, confusion and torment fill this young girls little head.

I want to run and get rid of this pain, if I left this very moment I'd never be back, I just can't remain.

In a home where happiness and love don't exist, no memory of good times, just what have I've missed?

My dad says it's my fault and his anger he'll blame, on a young girl who's clueless, yet carries his shame.

If I hadn't been born my mother would be, content and happy then and without me.

I am so bad I can't understand why, I wish I were gone now or maybe to die.

The tears will not stop now and I'm in need of love, I open my eyes you're here this very moment and with me above.

I feel content and safe now, I know its okay. Tomorrow will come…and with you beside me I drift away.

FOOTPRINTS IN THE SAND

One night I dreamed I was walking along the beach with the Lord. Many scenes from my life flashed across the sky. In each scene I noticed footprints in the sand. Sometimes there were two sets of footprints, other times there were one set of footprints. This bothered me because I noticed that during the low periods of my life, when I was suffering from anguish, sorrow or defeat, I could see only one set of footprints. So I said to the Lord, "You promised me Lord, that if I followed you, you would walk with me always. But I have noticed that during the most trying periods of my life there have only been one set of footprints in the sand. Why, when I needed you most, you have not been there for me?" **The Lord replied, "The times when you have seen only one set of footprints, is when I carried you."**

By Mary Stevenson, 1936

FOREVER AT MY SIDE

Your love is my life Lord, my future in your hands. I've given up control now and welcome your command.

So many things have changed for me it's hard to clearly see, my option now is transparent to trust and to believe.

For you almighty Father will surely take my hand, to walk this final step in life, you guide me with your wisdom into the promised land.

I have no fear, for what happens I know your words are true. I'll make these alterations in life, I can, for I have you.

2 Timothy 1:3 - I thank God, whom I serve, as my ancestors did, with a clear conscience, as night and day I constantly remember you in my prayers.

FORGIVE

When crisis comes into your life and you are
in despair, you can't always tell someone how it hurts and
do not want to share.

We pray to find the answer and hope that Christ will see,
how much you need His help, to live your destiny.

Free of pain and worry, your commitment to a better life.
Hands raised in praise of Christ today, a better
understanding of right and wrong, as we continue on our
way.

To trespass and be un-Christ like is not a conscious part,
your tomorrows and today's are felt inside your heart.

To be forgiven and to forgive will only make it right, ask
for blessings and you will find the answers, as you kneel in
prayer tonight.

I am sorry for my sins and forgive those who have sinned
against me seems, its' difficult to do. It takes a bigger
person to forgive and to be forgiven, a choice that's up to
you.

Your life can be like His if you understand His ways, to
walk His road and find His way for the remainder of your
days.

Exodus 32:32- Yet now, If thou wilt forgive their sin; and if not, blot me, I pray thee, out of thy book which thou hast written

HEAVENLY FATHER

Heavenly Father, I'm now all alone in a place full of memories that we called home.

Every corner I turn I see him/her here, I can carry on as one without any fear.

There are pictures and things within these four walls, my energy is drained as evening falls.

I haven't been alone for forty plus years, I'm confused and overwhelmed now overcome with my tears.

Give me the courage and faith that I need, to challenge myself as one going forward alone indeed.

Although his/her death is something I never expected, we all can stand tall and be resurrected. I am strong and capable of handling my life; I can do it well without any strife.

I will continue to listen and know when I pray, you are walking beside me every day.

You won't let me falter and won't let me fail, the future is mine and your love prevails.

Leviticus 26:12 - I will walk among you and be your God, and you will be my people.

TO GO FORWARD

For any wrong that's done there should be right, amidst the darkness there is always light.

And when the world comes crashing down on you don't despair, Our Lord and Savior is always there.

To pick you up and nurture you, with all hopelessness He will see you through.

To a brighter day where you can be, positive and hopeful for all to see.

When the clouds of doubt are gone from sight, you accomplished this with strength and hope and learned how to fight.

For what is right and always just, believe and be courageous and always trust.

The Lord wants you to walk with him, with faith, love, commitment, and void of sin.

A peaceful world awaits us all as we unite, to be of his likeness and wait for the light.

He loves us and welcomes the cleansed and the pure, He will be there in glory we all can be sure.

CAN YOU HEAR ME FATHER

Can you hear me Father? I am needing you today. Wipe my tears away, help me understand, can you hear me as I pray?

I know there is a reason; I need to walk this path.
I believe the words you gave us and know you have a plan; I want to leave the future and our fate within your mighty hands.

You make decisions for our life and guide us every day, to listen and to make the right choices as we go on our way.

I have always had a picture of how my life would be, I never questioned that it would play out as my reality.

And now I have a challenge to understand and to let go, your plan, although it's different, is all I need to know.

I know there is a reason; I need to walk this path.
I am struggling now for answers and want to take control, yet once I let your way take its course, I know I will be whole.

To follow this road I am walking now and to trust I will be fine, to know you're always with me and to know your love divine.

I will not be alone to struggle or fight to once again control, I give my faith completely to you, I will be whole.

2 Corinthians 1:4 - *who comforts us in all our troubles, so that we can comfort those in any trouble with the comfort we ourselves receive from God.*

YOU ARE MY STRENGTH

Today I live with faith that you are always here with me. I cannot comprehend those blind that cannot see.

That everything in life that's good is surely your creation. That each and every man has choice in each and every nation.

To honor you, to follow you, and to spread the truth. Your words and love you demonstrate surely as our proof.

And when those angry who live with hate invade our sacred space, what can we do as Christians to guard and protect our faith?

If we can march as Christians and go up against our foe, with God's love as our weapon to spread to all we know.

And though some feel fearful and doubt that he will be there to march right beside us for everyone to see.

He believes the world is worth our efforts in each and every case. For we can share His power no issues with those who love, without concern for any race.

His faith in all is everything and He will fight until the end. To humble all his servants to offer them as friends.

For only in His numbers can our lives be free. To spread His love and truth for all eternity.

And once our days are over and the end is very near. Stand strong; profess your love for God go forward without fear.

HIS LIGHT WILL NEVER DIM

Each day as I awaken I thank the Lord for what today will bring. I count my blessings and look to Him, His teachings are everything.

My heart rejoices as I look for joy and contemplate this great new day. Without our Father in my life, I would walk a very lonely path without purpose along the way.

My life is very complete as I give praise to Christ my savior, with my love and trust in Him I will never waver.

He gives life true meaning to His people and clearly leads their way. A bond of Christianity and righteousness for His humble servants, each and every day.

When you awake tomorrow with love, please pledge to walk Him. Your life will hold the answers and His light will never dim.

Luke 11:36 - Therefore, if your whole body is full of light, and no part of it dark, it will be just as full of light as when a lamp shines its light on you."

I WILL WALK WITH GOD

I will walk with you every step of the way; I have nothing to fear any time of the day.

Your loss won't burden you one minute too long, if you can let me carry you until you are strong.

Your loved one is fine now and exempt from all pain, they are no longer crippled and feeling disdain.

A new day was waiting with God at their side, their lives would be different they thought now with pride.

Acceptance they rendered while waiting for time to end on this earthly plain, to stand with the others who had left from whence they came.

The light it grew brighter and they reached out their hand, to welcome the new life and be able to stand on their own once again.

Void of limitations and such, to feel dignity in God's Kingdom they have wanted so much.

It's time to take notice and know they are fine, let loneliness and sorrow pass now, it's time.

LOVE

It is my nature to love.

The love of God flows through my heart to the hearts of others. When I am a conduit for love, I recognize the divinity in all beings. I honor their lives and want only the best for them.

Following the teaching of Jesus and to love one another is easy when I cherish people dear to me. However, I am also called to appreciate those who are different from me, and even those who hurt or offend me. Loving as Jesus loved means to accept all people as expressions of Spirit, regardless of their actions, choices, or abilities. They are the beloved of God.

Love lives in me. It flows from Spirit and I share it with others. As I love, I am fully alive. I love because it is my nature to love.

John 13:34 – A new command I give you: Love one another. As I have loved you, so you must love one another.

MARCH WITH ME

March forward with me and speak only God's truth, spread goodness and faith you have all the proof.

For those who cannot see that I am always there, whenever they struggle I will answer their prayers.

You have witnessed my love and heard what I say, I have given you trust and will show you the way.

For when two or more gather in my Holy name, all glory and wisdom is theirs to proclaim.

My words and my guidance will certainly be their shield and their sword in adversity.

There will be no darkness for those who believe, some question this concept and cannot perceive.

That by example I have shown who I am, with courage, and forgiveness I have taken my stand.

Against those who have evil intent, I will not give up and will not relent.

For I am a child of our almighty God, I will walk with all who follow where others have trod.

Take up your masses and let them all know, they won't be abandoned wherever they go.

With truth and repentance this world can heal, take the first step today and I will reveal.

The glory and wonder of life for all those who believe find strength and commitment and walk with me.

Those who walk with God, always reach their destination.

2 Corinthians 5:20 - We are therefore Christ's ambassadors, as though God were making his appeal through us. We implore you on Christ's behalf: Be reconciled to God.

MARCH WITH GOD

I want to spread your glory, I want to spread your truth, we need to have your love prevail for love they cannot refute.

So many now are wandering in search of something good, yet are they looking at Our Father's love I wish they would.

I cannot watch the actions of the devil in despair, so many things are wrong; it seems so hard to bear.

The devils work is rampant and causing life to be chaotic, with contempt and greed not good for you and me.

The world in total uproar now with anger and hate at the helm, it's time to take his words and love rise up, we can overwhelm!

So march with the sacred unity go up against the foe, with kindness, understanding, and love as our sword and shield, God Our Father can win I know.

HELMET of Salvation
BREASTPLATE of Righteousness
put on the armour
clothe yourselves with the Lord Jesus Christ
SHIELD of Faith BELT of Truth
SWORD of the Word
SANDALS of Peace

Ephesians 6:10-18- Finally, my brethren, be strong in the Lord, and in the power of his might. Put on the whole armour of God, that ye may be able to stand against the wiles of the devil. For we wrestle not against flesh and blood, but against principalities, against powers, against the rulers of the darkness of this world, against spiritual wickedness in high places. Wherefore take unto you the whole armour of God, that ye may be able to withstand in the evil day, and having done all, to stand. Stand therefore, having your loins girt about with truth, and having on the breastplate of righteousness; And your feet shod with the preparation of the gospel of peace; Above all, taking the shield of faith, wherewith ye shall be able to quench all the fiery darts of the wicked. And take the helmet of salvation, and the sword of the Spirit, which is the word of God.

MIRACLES

Do you believe in miracles? Do they happen every day? Are miracles inspired just by those who kneel and pray?

When crisis situations are knocking at your door, can a miracle take place? Can you count on more?

I've had a chance to look at miracles and see them every day, the miracle of love or in clouds so far away.

The budding of a cherry tree, the soaring of a bird, a smile upon a baby's face, with just a quiet word.

Awakening every morning and breathing life's sweet air, when troubles arise a friend naught say, you know they care.

The thrill of special holidays with friends and family, the warm and tender feelings, a child upon your knee.

A sun that is rising in the east and giving light too day, the smile from a stranger passing by as you go on your way.

Joy from the life you're given with every passing day, can we doubt all these miracles, perhaps we shouldn't try?

Recognize God's true blessings and see them all to be, great miracles he's given to all both to you and me.

And now let's take a moment; reflect on all these things, for miracles take place daily, praise God for all he brings.

***Galatians* 3:5-** *He therefore that ministereth to you the Spirit, and worketh miracles among you, doeth he it by the works of the law, or by the hearing of faith*

OUR LORD AND SAVIOR

Lord Jesus, our savior your birth came tonight, brought to this earth to make sure things are right.

Some of us know you and the sacrifice you made, for each of your children their sins you forgave.

Yet others still wander with fears and despair, they just cannot see the hardship you bear.

You faced such a challenge when subjected to your foe, yet you did it with courage, your sacrifice for all to know.

As we stand before you to face our own fate, will we do it in worship and love or face life with hate.

Hate for our kindred and hate for each other, deny the great wisdom from our Lord and our Father.

Each day you remind us of the miracles you gave, with the hope that your children their lives you could save.

If we all can bear witness and trust life to be, a true gift from our Lord Jesus for both you and me.

So rise up, and take notice that He paved the way, for heaven awaits those who worship in pursuit of His truth every day.

We were all created in His image and likeness, free from all sin, walk forward as Gods child and walk with Him.

PRAISE GOD AND HIS GLORY

When you speak his name speak loud and speak clear, don't whisper so quiet that no one can hear.

He gives love and glory to all who will ask; don't worship in silence for it's not a task.

To praise and give thanks for the blessings bestowed, to all who believe and all who will know.

That our Heavenly Father created us all, to walk tall and proud even if we fall.

He's there to carry us held in his arms, safe from all evil and to avoid any harm.

He believes all are worthy of his love and his trust, to kneel and pay homage for we surely must.

Give credit to Our Father, His only Son; at all times remember when the day is done.

He provides us always with his holy truth, it's there for the taking , it's the only truth.

John 8:32 - "If you continue in My word, then you are truly disciples of Mine; 3and you will know the truth, and the truth will make you free."

The wonders and glory the greatest of all, for all to bear witness and answer his call.

Believe and rejoice in his holiness, repent for your sins and you will be blessed.

With blue skies and the wonders of life just out your back door, he shows love and mercy can we want for much more?

So take precious time now and give thanks right now, for all that he has given and if all will allow.

His goodness and love will shine bright with each day, be faithful and loving whenever you pray.

We are his children he vows to lead, to our great tomorrow for this all can believe.

2 Peter 3:18 - *But grow in the grace and knowledge of our Lord and Savior Jesus Christ. To him be glory both now and forever! Amen.*

THE PATH YOU CHOOSE

The life you live depends on the choices you make and the path you choose, it's looking at your future and what you stand to gain or if you will lose.

And where does our Father fit into your life, a life filled with goodness and love or a life full of strife.

To be clear and focused on your needs, walking your path, just where does it lead?

To a life of fulfillment with self-centered goals, or a life full of joy , the Lords work, and all that it holds.

The choice is all yours and your past can include, a change in direction that you thought you would elude.

Without cause or caring from wince you came, to worship and praise and speak His name.

The Lord Jesus Christ is waiting for all, to live by goodness and truth, and to answer his call.

As you think of your choices you need to remember, the blessing of life that comes each December.

We all are born a life as innocent beings; recognize your blessing today the gift of believing.

The glory and wonder of our great Creator, when choosing your path don't wait until later.

Without goodness and truth your present can be, empty and fruitless for all to see.

I urge you, think wisely and make the right choice. The right path is there for you …. To give praise and rejoice.

On this road of great glory the path clearly leads, to offer up answers and resolve your needs.

To live as Gods child and be truly blessed, with God and our savior Lord Jesus, this path is best.

For you and his children to follow with care, to live by his words, a life blessed in good deeds and constant prayer. To Our Father, His Son our Savior.

Jeremiah 11:6 - The LORD said to me, "Proclaim all these words in the towns of Judah and in the streets of Jerusalem: 'Listen to the terms of this covenant and follow them.

YOUR REWARD

We all have wants and needs in life, we all have hopes and dreams.

We all need reinforcement and praise for what we do, the pride of this accomplishment is not enough it seems.

Why do we feel inadequate and look for others praise, is there a selfish need for what we do each and every day?

Why can't we simply feel proud of ourselves and what we have become.

And love ourselves for who we are, not look for praise from anyone.

If everything you do today is given from your heart, it will only be perceived as kind and what a place to start.

Our Father has no agenda for the love that He gives.

No hidden need for things, you will feel the pureness of this gift and what love from Him will always bring.

And you will praise Our Father with adoration and He will clearly feel, that everything he did that day His love and truth to all revealed.

I believe that if we live as He lives and give without a need of praise.

Our reward is knowing that love was given as He would give, our reward for every day.

And when the day is ended and you feel you have given love to all who are in need.

Take pride in who you are, and know that God's love is your reward and God is all you need.

To be that special person you have been looking for in life, know that you are a child of God and love yourself, give thanks and praise to God each and every night.

TO LIVE AS YOUR FAITHFUL SERVANT

My life is in chaos and I am fearful of today, Father are you with me and do you hear me as I pray.

I am waiting for your answers and cannot move ahead, until I hear you speak to me I will live within this dread.

For a future without purpose and void of my lifelong mate, will my prayers be answered, or is it just too late?

All your lessons urge us to follow you and to believe in the miracles of life you offer.

To give now, not to receive.

For when we walk as you would walk and spread your love to all, we are certain to walk with you with a promise we will not fall.

And as we are your soldiers, to fight against our foe, are you present with us Lord to guide us where to go.

The heroes sent before us who fought to do your work. Are with you once again, their example not to shirk.

For each of us should recognize and know that we are strong. If motivated and with reverence to you this battle will not be long.

For once your truth and love are spoken and clearly heard by those, that you are here for us with words that you have chose.

To live a life that's sweet and pure enveloped with your love, will find answers there from your Kingdom up above.

And when we feel your presence and practice every day, to all we know and meet not only when we pray.

With praise and with honor I am your servant Lord, I cannot doubt your lessons, your love surely is The Word.

So, as I sit and wonder what am I to do, I know my future in this life is clearly one with you.

THE SECRET PLACE

There's a secret place within your soul where wondrous things begin.

We keep them locked within ourselves as though it were a sin.

To have our feelings known by all, to trust our inner self.

To love, believe, and trust to truly share our wealth.

I've wondered oh so many times and often question why?

Should it be right to thank, rejoice and not okay to cry?

We stifle feelings all the time and bottle them inside. How can we know and feel these things, not relish them with pride.

Yet deep inside our soul we know that we should display the goodness.

Love and truth we know, each second of the day.

The world today is often full of sadness and despair, give thanks, rejoice, praise God today, and let the trumpets blare.

No secrets hidden from the world, our inner selves alive.

I know we will adjust to love, belief and goodness, but uppermost to trust.

THE WONDER OF TODAY

I have loved with true conviction, I will love without prediction.

With innocence and with hope for tomorrow, I take these vows to love and will never borrow.

Hopes and dreams for our forever, a love that is timeless. Without boundaries or barriers, to carry us through the good and the bad. Today, tomorrow and forever, yet today life has awakened once more.

Hopes, dreams and love within my reach, all right here to learn and teach.

My family, friends and for those who care, God's love and his presence are always there.

No matter what our days unfold, cherish memories, make dreams come true, and live life with God and do behold, the wonder of today………

Genesis 1:28 - *God blessed them and said to them, "Be fruitful and increase in number; fill the earth and subdue it. Rule over the fish in the sea and the birds in the sky and over every living creature that moves on the ground."*

TRUTH & LIGHT

It's a miracle to me the way my life to date has evolved,
from a child weak and fragile, to a woman with resolve.

My road as it continues complete with love and prayer,
when changes happen daily I know that you are there.

My journey has been good to me and I welcome more, I
cannot predict my future, and don't know what's in store.

For only God Our Father knows what tomorrow will bring
my way, I always find peace and patience when I kneel and
pray.

I give my heart and soul to Him for he will guide me
through, regardless of the outcome I will always come
home to you.

You are my strength and hope today you will always be,
the truth and light I need for life and always there for me.

Today I worship and give thanks and praise to Thee,
Our Father, Son, and Spirit forever standing hand in hand
with me.

Micah 4:5- All the nations may walk in the name of their gods, but we will walk in the name of the LORD our God forever and ever.

TOGETHER

Hold my hand and walk with me feel His love and grace, bask in His kindness and His goodness let them see upon your face.

You are a child of God and will relinquish need for wrong, for God has given His beauty in faith, blue skies, perhaps within a song.

Proclaiming all His wonders and the love we have for Him, let go of any darkness, let go of all your sin.

Lift your voice in worship for all the world to hear, transfer the joy of life to all especially those that you hold dear.

Surround yourself with those who know that God is love, and always walk with your head lifted to His light above.

For anyone who chooses to live life precariously, and cast their fate to those corrupt and live with greed and hate, is not for you and me.

I choose to find my comfort in a kind heart and those who know; that God has lived a life fulfilled and will continue to show.

Each of us the way to truth and peace within our days, read His words and know His love and always give him praise.

For those who do not demonstrate unconditional love for Him and know His world of brightness, will choose to live in sin.

So as you walk together with those who are reverent and vow to live, a life that follows His path for us a life that's void of evil and of sin.

***2 John 1:4**- It has given me great joy to find some of your children walking in the truth, just as the Father commanded us.*

WALK WITH ME

Walk with me, live as I live. Forgive those who have sinned against you, and you shall be forgiven.

Do not sit in judgment; I cannot accept blame or finding fault with others.

I have given you tools and my words in which to live.

We are all accountable for our actions.

Life is a lesson for all to learn.

Give love to all, as you are loved.

Do not be fearful, love can conquer all.

Worship, and respect my words, they are your textbook for life.

There will be a day of reckoning, the time is coming for all to stand together and witness my true love.

Be patient and kind to your fellow man, let your love shine.

Help those who are in need, as I hold your hand on this journey hold theirs.

ANNE AWBREY

WALK WITH THE LORD

As the potter spins his wheel his creation will take form, when the Lord cries out to us we should conform.

To his great words of wisdom that are there for us each day, at night we can be grateful, to give thanks as we kneel to pray.

For we are his creation his love and trust are there, to live a life free of sin, a life beyond compare.

Our work can be difficult with the world the way it is, commit to Christ our Savior and proclaim that you are His.

To walk a road as he would walk and live your life for him, a life that's pure and free of corruption from sin.

And as the years pass by us we will past the test, for God our Heavenly Father waits to welcome us home some day and He will do the rest.

As the gates open to you do not be afraid, the light is shining on you and your choice was made.

To walk the road with Him, your journey will begin, free of all impurities and free from any sin.

Rejoice and sing his praise with all who want you to, it's your reward to be with God it's what he wants for you.

WHY BELIEVE?

How can I doubt you, your goodness, and your truth? You exhibit your love and have given us proof.

You sacrificed your Son, with example to set, to spread your word, true lessons to learn, yet often they just are not heard.

What gives us the option not to believe, we walk with needs and ego right on our sleeve.

Help me Lord Jesus how can I see, the meaning in life, what's right for me?

I don't have to look far to find where you are, you walk with your children and never are far.

Away from your children who worship and live, by your commandments blessed by all that you give.

They should not be altered to suit you and I, for God's goodness and truth we cannot deny.

Come from a life that's lived as you command, you give us a choice you never demand.

But soon we will witness the pain in your heart, of those who deny you and are apart.

Of heathens' and those chosen to change your path, who create mass corruption hence life filled with great wrath?

It's time to take notice repent for our sins, walk with courage together or evil will win.

I will walk with you Lord and be by your side, forever to know you to experience great pride.

And by your example will live by your word, and will spread love and goodness when I am heard.

You have helped me through peril and times of great pain; I would never leave you or live with distain.
For my Lord and Savior Jesus Christ, My God.

Galatians 3:5 - So again I ask, does God give you his Spirit and work miracles among you by the works of the law, or by your believing what you heard?

YOU ARE NOT ALONE

Where you walk I walk with you.
You are not alone….

When you speak I will speak.
You are not alone….

In the quiet of your day you can hear me, be still and it will be.
You are not alone….

When your heart aches I will comfort you.
You are not alone….

Cherish today and embrace the moment, listen for my words.
You are not alone….

You cannot lose me for I am always here.
You are not alone….

Believe in who you are and know that you are strong.
You are not alone….

Do not speculate on tomorrow, live in today.
You are not alone…

When you are weak I will carry you.

When you are fearful I will give you hope.

When you are tired I will rest with you.
You are not alone….

As you face tomorrow I will face it with you, listen for my words.
You are not alone….

The Father, the Son, and the Holy Spirit are here with you.
You are not alone….

Be grateful for what you have and ask for what you need.
A grain of sand is worth more than an ounce of gold.
Embrace the day and go forward knowing
You are not alone….

I am here with you always, listen for my words.

John 10:28 - *I give them eternal life, and they shall never perish; no one will snatch them out of my hand.*

YOUR PROMISE FOREVER

A little child lost and confused I looked for the truth, mixed messages were nothing in life so I searched for the proof.

That God would protect me and keep me from harm, I grew to adulthood a true broken soul I sensed with alarm.

There are many souls out there in need of healing, who wander in confusion without love or feeling?

The need to embrace Him and turn life around, to listen for guidance and just hear the sound.

Of His voice so clear I follow his path for living, to not sit in judgment and be forgiving.

Not just for others but for your sins as well, He sacrificed his life and came back to tell.

That this life is a struggle but your way will be clear, if you walk close beside me I'm sure you will hear.

Testimony and proof that your life will be, courageous and fulfilling a true tribute to Thee.

And as I move forward I desperately need, for my life with you present is foremost for me.

I am willing to listen and to learn to walk next to Thee, the road rough and rocky for both you and me.

But your peril and pain your cause to guide so plain to see, your children who sin and live life with impurities.

You'll call them and urge them to fall to their knees, to witness your love and constantly plea.

To live with conviction and follow your lead, for our true salvation is all that we need.

So shout the words clearly, give unto the Lord.

YOUR WAY IS MY WAY

Your way is my way, it's clear to me now; I've needed control and yet never knew how.

I could manage my life and have it be, the way that I wanted designed to please me.

And then things were altered along the way, my life changed drastically in just one day.

I realized then as I realize now, I cannot control your plan Lord I just don't know how.

I relinquished myself to you and the way became clear, if I listened and believed the answers were here.

I can and I will with you at my side, close to me now Lord and you are my guide.

I trust and believe that I can go on now, to trust and believe and this I do vow.

I hear the words clearly I believe what I hear,
Our Father, the Son, and the Holy Spirit will lead me, there is nothing to fear.

Exodus 15:2- "The LORD is my strength and my defense; he has become my salvation. He is my God, and I will praise him, my father's God, and I will exalt him.

ANNE AWBREY

CAN YOU HEAR ME FATHER

Can you hear me Father? I am needing you today.
Wipe my tears away; help me understand, can you hear me as I pray?

I know there is a reason; I need to walk this path
I believe the words you gave us and know you have a plan.
I want to leave the future and our fate within your mighty hands.

You make decisions for our life and guide us every day, to listen and to make the right choices as we go on our way.

I have always had a picture of how my life would be, I never questioned that it would play out as my reality.

And now I have a challenge to understand and to let go, your plan, although it's different, is all I need to know.

I know there is a reason; I need to walk this path.
I am struggling now for answers and want to take control, yet once I let your way take its course I know I will be whole.

To follow this road I am walking now and to trust I will be fine, to know you're always with me and to know your love divine. I will not be alone to struggle or fight to once again control, I give my faith completely with you I will be whole.

OUR GREATEST FEAR

It is our light not our darkness that most frightens us.
Our deepest fear is not that we are inadequate.
Our deepest fear is that we are powerful beyond measure.

It is our light not our darkness that most frightens us.
We ask ourselves, who am I to be brilliant, gorgeous, talented, and fabulous? Actually, who are you not to be? You are a child of God.

Your playing small does not serve the world. There is nothing enlightened about shrinking so that other people want feel insecure around you. We were born to make manifest the glory of God that is within us. It's not just in some of us; it's in everyone.

And as we let our own light shine, we unconsciously give other people permission to do the same. As we are liberated from our own fear, Our presence automatically liberates others.

By Marianne Williamson

TO SAY GOODBYE

It's time to let you go….

Goodbye my love and God speed, you have been everything in life to me.

I will go on with courage and faith.

A promise I make with my love, I'll feel you and know you are with me in heaven above.

We met long ago and shared wedding vows, for good times and bad times in sickness and health.

We have been blessed on this journey in life with a wealth of memories to last us forever…….

So for the time being I can let you go, in eternity together someday we both know.

Until then my darling I will miss you forever, rest now in peace and your suffering is over.

John 14:23- Jesus replied, "Anyone who loves me will obey my teaching. My Father will love them, and we will come to them and make our home with them.

FEAR OF TOMORROW

I know your fear, I know your pain, and I have walked your road before. In the midst of sadness I knew there would be more.

I've cried your tears so many times and often felt despair, this hand that had been dealt to me was wrong and so unfair.

I had no hope I didn't care my life was over then, no will to face tomorrow I'd never be happy again.

A constant state of fog prevailed each and every day, to think about a future alone I pondered in dismay.

I couldn't think, I couldn't plan, and had no inner drive. He was gone, I missed him so, and why was I alive?

The hours and days passed an answer yet to find, the sun would shine, I'd hear the birds, and yet I was so blind.

To feel that sweet tomorrow as life proceeds each day, to take a breathe and stand as one to never look away.

I had a life, I have a life it's changed somewhat it seems. I lived a life, yet will go on with brand new hopes and dreams

For like they say life changes without a guarantee, to anyone that you can count on, just what you want to see.

It's hard to see tomorrow without the one you love, if you believe and trust in God …HE listens from above.

Genesis 50:19- And Joseph said unto them, Fear not: for am I in the place of God

GUIDANCE

On bended knees let me comfort you, I feel your weakness and will get you through.

This trying time you are living right now, with my love and guidance I will not allow.

The pain and hurt to remain a part, of your lonely soul and aching heart.

A bright new future is within your reach; I have helped many others and will continue to teach.

A way to heal and forge ahead in my glory, to change your path and to share your story.

With others who are lost and looking for light, to get through the pain and get through their plight.

As there is always an answer when life becomes dark, be trusting, courageous and listen to your heart.

My words are there just listen and you will hear, they'll chase off the evil and diminish your fear.

A bright new tomorrow is outside your door, just listen and know that you will learn so much more.

My words they were written with lost souls in mind, be gentle, be patient, give love and be kind.

To all those that love you and who are right by your side, hold hands, be quiet and listen for I am your guide.

Into your life and for all your tomorrows, I'll teach and be there for you each day as they follow.

Your commitment to believe and hear what I say, your past and your present and all of today.

We'll walk together and your life will be, fulfilling and blessed if you stand as one right here with me.

Deuteronomy 32:37- And he shall say, Where are their gods, their rock in whom they trusted

I GIVE MY HEART

It's a miracle to me the way my life to date has evolved, from a child weak and fragile to a woman with resolve.

My road as it continues complete with love and prayer, when changes happen daily I know that you are there.

My journey has been good to me and I welcome more, I cannot predict my future and don't know what's in store.

For only God Our Father knows what tomorrow will bring my way, I always find peace and patience when I kneel and pray.

I give my heart and soul to Him for he will guide me through, regardless of the outcome I will always come home to you.

You are my strength and hope today and you will always be, the truth and light I need for life and always there for me.

Today I worship and give thanks and praise to Thee, Our Father, Son, and Spirit forever standing hand in hand with me.

ANNE AWBREY

MY CHILD MY ANGEL

Our Father in heaven I don't understand, as I walk down the hall my child's hand in my hand.

We're here for your treatment they'll push, prod and check you, your eyes well with tears yet there's nothing I can do.

I whisper be brave it soon will be done; my heart is so heavy for my little one.

The courage you show a true miracle to me, how can this be happening and how can it be.

For I am the parent who's lived many years, I'll give you my love and wipe away your tears.

I'll pray when I'm with you and not leave your side, Our father in heaven will be my guide.

So innocent and frail at this time in your life, to live with this illness to live with this strife.

Not knowing your future just to live for this day, no time for tomorrow but just for today.

The pain and the unknown of this dreaded disease, I pray every second you walk with God and will walk with ease.

You have given such joy and love to us all, we can't watch you suffer we can't watch you fall.

I pray Holy Father please help us to be strong, to cherish the time we have with our child no matter how long.

To know when your eyes close with a final good-bye, that God is with you always and there is no need to cry.
In your short existence as an angel you came, and while with us did Gods work in His holy name.

Our lives will continue your memory won't dim, you are free to be happy to romp and to play, the pain and the suffering have gone away.

You are with your creator forever our child, the greatest gift of love we had for awhile. We need to be thankful and trust you will be a loving angel in heaven as you walk with Thee.

MY EVENING PRAYER

Our Father in heaven. Thank you for my yesterdays, my todays, and for my tomorrow. *My prayer each and every night.*

Throughout my life I have been hit hard and knocked down to my knees; I have cried a million tears and prayed for God to help me to be strong and to walk through life with ease.

I have wallowed in self-pity and envied those around, prayers that were spoken privately unanswered without a sound.

The final blow that left me standing all alone, was the day I lost my partner now standing by myself (I thought) in our empty home.

The quiet was too quiet and I felt the void each day, of laughter and love with my tomorrows on their way.

I need to take a break I thought and to familiarize, to bask in the sun, to read His words, to look into His eyes..

Then on a bright and sunny morning while praying once again, I heard his gentle words to me and knew I was with Him.

He spoke of walking with me and listening for his voice the answers are right there, just believe the words I've written as you kneel in prayer.

From that day forward I will hear Him say, just be still and listen when you kneel and pray.

The answers and your future are resting in my hands; if you believe and follow me together we can stand.

We look to brighter days ahead feeling hopeful and secure, that life will bring you happiness a promise true and pure.

My life is new today and tomorrow it has come, I found a love, I have a life, and His will for me was done.

Once again such happiness and once again deep love, I owe to Christ our Lord, our Savior, and our Father from above.

He is the force behind me now and I would like to share, His words, His love, and promise for a life complete are beyond compare.

1 Kings 9:3- The LORD said to him: "I have heard the prayer and plea you have made before me; I have consecrated this temple, which you have built, by putting my Name there forever. My eyes and my heart will always be there.

MY WALK ALONE

Our Father in heaven you hear me I know, He's failing each day now and I can't let go.

I'm doing my best lord and wanting to feel, it's in your hands now but it's all so surreal.

My family and friends support me each day, I'm groping for answers to have it my way.

Reality has never been important to me, I've had it my way the way it should be.

We've reached an age now where time seems to fly; I'm not finished living so why should my loved one die.

I keep looking for guidance from sources and have yet to find, an answer to ease my mind.

Fear is so constant and with me each day, please help me accept this I continue to pray.

I know that our future you hold in your hands, your words were spoken and your truth still stands.

I will continue to listen and can accept, our journey together will end soon without regret.

The pain and the hopelessness will end for you; Gods will can prevail now I know this to be true.

We've shared a lifetime together I'm grateful for that; I'll walk with God now without you and be strong in my faith. Until my time is over and I'm on my way to be with you forever.

PREPARED FOR TOMORROW

You pain is my pain, your fear is my fear, I need you today, I need you tomorrow, I just need you near.

And when the day comes and you're taken home, I know with God's love I am never alone.

The good times, the bad times will always be, just a moment away in my memory.

I vowed to you then, I vow to you now, as life goes on for me I will survive somehow.

I cannot question why I only know today, tomorrow is forever though you are far away.

I hold on to the goodness and hold on to the love, that brought us together a blessing from above.

Our father walks with me and won't let me fall; with courage and God's love I know I'll stand tall.

Prepared for tomorrow and prepared for today, he's holding my hand now and won't let me stray.

Job 28:27- then he looked at wisdom and appraised it; he confirmed it and tested it.

UNTIL WE MEET AGAIN

I listen to the silence and somehow hear the noise, know the deepest sorrow, yet feel the greatest joy.

I experience the darkness while standing in the light, as the sun embraces my body in the middle of the night.

My whisper of your name at night echoes loudly in the hills, the thunderous sound of rainstorms so peaceful and so still.

The tears I shed in sorrow pass the smile upon my lips, the emptiness at night alone still feels your fingertips.

My heart so sadly broken awaits the bright new day, I will feel your presence always although you've passed away.

Rest with God's love Chuck, as I drift to sleep tonight. Until we meet again

Matthew 18:4 - Therefore, whoever takes the lowly position of this child is the greatest in the kingdom of heaven.

A FIVE YEAR OLDS FEAR

It's late at night and Mommy says to hide, I find the couch and curl up in a little ball right alongside.

And in he comes this angry man, to hurt my Mommy as he always can.

She's bleeding and she's crying and begging him to stop, I'm quiet but I'm crying and cannot leave my spot.

He leaves the room its quiet now, but Mommy's crying badly. I don't know what to do for her, I huddle sadly.

If I'm quiet and I'm good and I'm pretty and I'm smart, can he ever find a place for me somewhere in his heart?

If I listen and I do what I should do, will he love me as my father the way I want him to?

My mother tries and tries and never pleases him, she takes abuse and pleads forgiveness for her every sin.

This has made him so very angry that he hurts and makes her bleed, and then he tells her that reason is because she gave birth to me.

Please help me dear Father to act the way I should, I know that I can please him if I am good.

A HEART AS GOOD AS GOLD

It all began in the forties a little girl was born, into a life both good and bad emotions would be torn.

For this little child a heart as good as gold, would ponder over love and hate her chapters yet untold.

And just like other children lessons to be taught, the ones we all must learn whether we like them or not.

Looking back at adolescent years, her lessons sometimes tough, from a mother's love abounding to her Dad's 'never enough'.

To see it now in retrospect her father loved her too, for he, his parent's only child, did the best that he could do.

When climbing to the teenage years her story still untold,
a semi-happy young woman now, a heart as good as gold.

Still searching for a happy place where special dreams come true. Looked high and low and up and down so she could be like you.

Content and happy, some rocky roads ahead with lessons left to learn. So restless and so discontent it had to cause concern.

And then one very special night a miracle took place
She met a man with sparkling eyes a smile upon his face.

His gentle ways, his laughter and unconditional love,
were truly like a gift from God, a blessing from above.

And here it is the nineties now; she's forty odd years old, content, fulfilled, and happy now with a heart as good as gold.

ALWAYS WITH ME

Why does this happen oh please let me hide, from the feelings I am feeling deep down inside.

My mother is crying and my father is mean, he hurts her so much I hear her screams.

I want to protect her but I am just small, I lay here in fear I hear it all.

Why does he hate us, I'm begging to know?

When he says he's leaving why he doesn't go?

I know you are here God please let me sleep, I feel so alone now I continue to weep.

As I lay here crying a miracle takes place, you're standing at my beside I clearly see your face.

You are here with me and I feel some relief, it's peaceful and quiet as I drift to sleep.

Tomorrow will come though and it could go either way, he'll be laughing and smiling or angry with rage.

But you will be with me I know that for sure, your words and your love God will make me secure.

I can continue this journey with hope and with prayer, I know you are with me and I know you'll be there.

Psalms 97:5 – *The hills melted like wax at the presence of the LORD, at the presence of the Lord of the whole earth.*

FRIEND

There is nothing you can't tell me I am always here; we have shared so many secrets over, oh so many years.

We've laughed and cried together so many times, it seems our friendship is nurtured with love and respect to share all of your dreams.

A friend is there forever and will never let you down, they can read your inner thoughts they know your smiles and frowns.

A sister born of the same name plays a special part, yet your friend is unconditional and will keep you in their heart.

Forever to be with you and keeps you close at hand, will love and listen to your dreams and always understand.

That special love that only comes to those, who feel and live with friendship even with the highs and lows. And you and I dear friend sisters of a different kind, we live apart today but are always close in mind.

John 15:13- Greater love hath no man than this, that a man lay down his life for his friends.

ANNE AWBREY

I'M SAFE WITH YOU HERE

Father In heaven I am waiting to hear, that you will protect me and banish all fear.

I lay in the darkness of my lonely room, I listen to fighting, this feels like a tomb.

Tear after tear fall as I lie in my bed, confusion and torment in this young girls head.

I want to run and get rid of this pain, I'd never come back it's so hard to remain.

In a home where happiness and love don't exist, no memory of good times, just what have I missed?

My dad says it's my fault and his anger he'll blame, on this scared little girl who carries his shame.

If I hadn't been born my mother would be, content and happy and without me.

I am so bad it seems I don't understand why, I wish I were not here or maybe to die.

The tears will not stop now and I need to be loved, I open my eyes you are here at this very moment from up above.

I feel content and safe now I know its okay, tomorrow will come and with you beside me I drift away.

ANNE AWBREY

TO CHANGE MY LIFE

I'm battered and bruised I have no self-worth. No joy or enjoyment no laughter, a life void of mirth.

I try desperately to call this our home, but somehow I'm always left here alone.

My children spend hours in fear of the night; you walk through the door and engage in a fight.

They love each of us and want to see, love and contentment in their family.

You are a monster, you're mean and unkind. You browbeat and torment without an ounce of remorse on your mind.

I know there is better for life to be had. You are not a husband, a friend, or a dad.

I pray every night that my prayers are heard, yet I still remain his victim and wait for His word.

I cannot pretend it all will all be fine; he'll kill me someday and leave orphans' behind.

I know I have options and need to react, we all can be safe and away from all that.

I am not going to let him take my strength from me,
I'll make it all happen and safe we will be.

I know God will help me and guide me today. I can
change my life, be strong, and I can get away.

From the sickness and torture we live every day, I
believe our Fathers love will come to those who pray.

And take charge of their lives who stand tall and
strong, to be in a world where we all belong.

WHO I AM

I am strong, I am wise, I am a child of God and don't deserve your rage. You constantly torment me and keep me captive like an animal in a cage.

I loved you so when we were wed and believed that we would be content.

To live a life with God from that moment on for all eternity.

You changed and you showed disrespect, with brutal acts of torture anytime you were mad.

My future threatened without joy, everything I valued had turned from good to bad.

It is apparent to everyone that something is very wrong, I need to pray and know that God can heal my spirit and make me strong.

Our children wonder frequently and live with frequent confusion, can Dad be such a monster or is this hate he has for us just a sick illusion?

I vowed at an early age to live a life fulfilled, to raise a family with love and happiness, no compromise for love.

Yet now I see that we have failed. I pray each night to God above to give me strength to help me fight, for freedom and a better life.

Without hurt or pain, I learn to laugh and dance again as I once did out in the rain.

I can and will change my life and create those happy days. For all of us deserve that right, we cannot live our lives in this dreadful daze.

If life is sad and painful for us without our Lord, I need to embrace His love and truth, to walk as a child of God.

To make my way without this angry man and follow in His footsteps on my journey forward.

A VICTIM NO MORE

As a child I was a victim of abuse long ago, with nowhere to hide and nowhere to go.

I lived in a home where evil prevailed, we were held there as prisoners and it was our jail.

To be held captive we couldn't be free, beatings and violence were frequent for my mother and me.

At first at a very young age it was Dad's belt, his presence evoked the fear and pain that was felt.

As I grew older the belt was replaced with hands and fists, flailing at my body and face.

His anger and rage were directed at us.

With wounds that were hidden there wasn't a trace.

The emotional wounds and scars could never heal, emotions that were hidden as though we didn't feel.

The torment and cruelty inflicted with rage, like animals huddled in his private cage.

For my mother and me there was no defense, it never seemed right and didn't make sense.

My brother was always a threat to my Dad; his masculinity was the weapon he had.

He was never a victim to the wrath of this man, he would go on his way and never would stand against this tyrant and horrible beast, it always confused me to say the least.

My perception was that he was the chosen one, the pride in Dad's eyes for he was the son.

Yet he suffered knowing what was happening when he would take off and leave us again and again.

And as time flew and years had passed by, I was a young woman and wished I could die.

I hated what was happening to my mother and me, if given the chance I would run far away until I was free.

And then my white knight came into my life.
We were married and betrothed as husband and wife.

Yet the scars and the memories remained in my mind
Of that terrible life I had left far behind.

I feared for my mother who was all alone now, I couldn't protect her I didn't know how.

I shared my deep secrets and worked with others to heal and forgive and to uncover.

The truth that I finally was safe, for he couldn't hurt me I was in a safe place.

At seventy years now I have to confess, I have let go of memories and fears and am finally at rest.

I miss both my parents and forgive them today, if you are a victim you can get away.

And spare pain for others in your family.

Take action and get out, you need to be free.

A victim no more who can stand on your own, to live as God wants you to in His happy home.

Praise Him and thank him for your time has come
No need for fear now…..No more to run.

GET HELP & GET OUT

Seventy years ago victims were limited without any type of options available for them. Very few safe refuge locations were available. Victims for the most part didn't have skills to become independent and find employment. In fact, many used this as an excuse to stay in the dysfunctional relationship.

There is no excuse for subjecting yourself or your family to abuse. There is no way that subjecting a child to abuse is acceptable. Painful acts and memories take years to overcome.

Find refuge and remove yourself and your family from harm's way. This is not love. The abuser in your life needs intense help.

THE NATIONAL DOMESTIC VIOLENCE HOTLINE

1-800-799-7233 | 1-800-787-3224 (TTY)

http://www.thehotline.org/

MY PROMISE

I kneel in prayer today dear Lord, and ask for forgiveness please. A troubled heart and soul I give, hands folded, my eyes looking up to you while resting on my knees.

I know there is an answer to the questions that I ask, I understand that you are here and I can face the task.

Of following you with confidence and knowing I will hear, your words and guidance on my path amidst the pain and fear.

I have lived for many years and asked for help along the way, have struggled with difficult situations and have reached my final days.

I can follow what I know to be the truth you share with those, who will listen as you speak to them to walk the path that you have chose.

From early years I know that God will make things right, that in the darkness as dawn awakes there always will be light.

In my last endeavor preparing for the day I leave this earthly plain, to live where truth and love prevail to a world that's free of pain.

As I walk these final steps toward home I know my life begins, when the doors will finally open to a life that's free from sin.

Until the final day is here, you have a promise that I will spread your love and goodness until the day I die.

Revelation 11:12 - Then they heard a loud voice from heaven saying to them, "Come up here." And they went up to heaven in a cloud, while their enemies looked on.

MY STORY

It has been my experience over the last sixty-five years that with the help of God, many painful events and traumas could be eliminated.

"Believe" are poems that I've written that embrace surrendering your life over to God. In all cases I have found that believing in Gods words, love, and guidance confirms that we are not alone in this journey of life. God is always there for us!

The poems titled "Grief," are poems that were written for individuals who suffer from the loss of a loved one.

"Abuse" is something that I encountered from an infancy stage. I truly connect with the emotional and physical abuse that people suffer from, because I lived with this "Abuse" through my entire childhood. By the grace of God, Our Father gave me hope, a vision. At an early age, I learned to surrender to God, which gave me the confidence to survive the abuse. I believe that there are many victims who are suffering from this kind of abuse. Out of fear I never felt comfortable discussing my situation with anyone. It has always been a goal of mine to enlighten those victims with the knowledge that they are never alone and that God is always with them. I managed to come through the years with superficial scars and a somewhat bruised spirit. I now realize that I always had Our Father right by my side and that I am a survivor.

I eventually was married and had three children of my own, although not perfect, very gratifying. My family struggled as most do. We suffered through the death of our parents and other loved ones. We also faced financial disaster as a result of two failed businesses. Twenty-seven years into our marriage, my husband was diagnosed with incurable non-Hodgkin's lymphoma and my sister was diagnosed with incurable brain cancer.

Yet with some counseling, a lot of determination, and Gods grace we survived as husband and wife, and parents for 34 years.

After my husband and sister were diagnosed with cancer, the next six and a half years would be a true test of my faith. I prayed, read Christian books, and communicated with God daily. Divine intervention and inspiration from God carried me once again. With strength given by God, I survived the death of my husband and sister with dignity and hope for tomorrow. Today, I am involved with a friend's journey with cancer and I know we will survive.

I am confident that my book can restore and in some cases, cultivate the same faith and love I have for God Our Father, his son Our Lord and Savior and the Holy Spirit. Without this love (surrender) I could not have survived and would not be living a happy and fulfilled life today. ***Surrender Today and Survive Tomorrow!***

God Bless,

Anne Awbrey

www.ingramcontent.com/pod-product-compliance
Lightning Source LLC
Chambersburg PA
CBHW071713040426
42446CB00011B/2039